The Fifth
And Far Finer
than the
First Four

637

Best Things
Anybody
Ever Said

THE FIFTH
And far finer than the than the first four

637

BEST THINGS ANYBODY EVER SAID

Presented with a
special bonus quote

Chosen and arranged by

Robert Byrne

Again

FAWCETT COLUMBINE · NEW YORK

For Cynthia
Who risked a postage stamp

When a thing has been said and well, have no scruple. Take it and copy it.

Anatole France
(1844–1924)

Contents

Introduction

Nobody is more surprised than I am to find myself standing before you with another collection of 637 mostly humorous quotations. "Haven't you already printed most of the good ones?" a friend asked gently after hearing the news. I wondered the same thing after each of the previous volumes. How many times can I milk this cow? is how I put it. Surely four is the limit, that being the number of spigots on the normal cow. But ever onward marches an army of comics, gag writers, cartoonists, wise apples, and philosophers, many of them amateurs, some of them as drab and ordinary, in fact, as you and I, but who nevertheless manage occasionally to extrude a gem. Every two or three or four years, apparently, the rampages of this humorous horde generate enough trash to enable a scavenger like me to fill a slim volume with glittering found objects.

My mother and father sacrificed a lot to send me through engineering school, and what did they get for their trouble? A gagpicker on the rubbish heap of humor. But happy! Quotes like #47 and #84, to spotlight only two out of 637, put me on the floor and should at least give you a snicker. Nothing quite compares with the shivers of pleasure I felt when I found the drawings for #350 and #487, to name two out of thirty-four.

Still, for a man with a certain natural grace and dignity, it is unsettling to see my name on the cover of a book whose index includes listings for Clap, Dork, Fresno, Ovary, Polyps, Scumbag, Upchuck, and Yuppies.

What are your criteria? a reader asks. How do you decide what to include? Those are impossible questions to answer, going as they do to the very core of my being, a hard, nut-like organ bathed in spleen and bile and best left uncracked. Looking at the results of my criteria—the book you hold in your hand—I'm embarrassed to see that I seem to find cynicism, pessimism, criticism, and negativism amusing, which is odd since in real life I am almost pathologically sweet. The quotes knocking Dan Quayle, for instance, while funny in a sense, I find a little too cruel for comfort. The office of the vice-presidency of the United States is one of the most prestigious in the world, and the man who once held it is deserving of a certain amount of respect even if he is a dim bulb.

Looking over all five collections of the 637 best things anybody ever said, certain trends emerge. Less is said now about smoking, drinking, and war than ten years ago, when I started in this dirty business. Remarks by Lenin and Trotsky have acquired an ironic patina. Words to live by and words of wisdom are in decline, offset by a rise in remarks about marriage, stupidity, and politics. Are these paradigm shifts or merely blips? The data are unscientific and readers are cautioned against using them as the basis for investment decisions.

As in the previous volumes, this one does not use the alphabet as a means of ordering subjects. Instead, the quotes are arranged whenever possible to mirror life. The book makes more sense if traversed from front to back. A typical sequence of subjects is Courtship, Love, Sex, Marriage, and Drink. Jews follow War; Boredom follows Celebrities; Lawyers follow Money; Stupidity follows Quayle.

My sincere thanks to the many readers who have taken the trouble to comment on my efforts and to submit lines for possible future editions. They are acknowledged by name in the Index of Sources (where my mailing address appears) and should be blamed for my shortcomings.

Robert Byrne
Petaluma, California

Part One

God and the Universe
Life Itself
Courtship and Love
Sex and Marriage
Drink
Birth
School
Men and Baldness
Men and Women
Cooking and Health
Age
Death
Animals

1

I'm worried that the universe will soon need replacing. It's not holding a charge.   *Edward Chilton*

2

Maybe this world is another planet's hell.
                                    Aldous Huxley (1894–1963)

3

They say that God is everywhere, and yet we always think of Him as somewhat of a recluse.
                                    Emily Dickinson (1830–1886)

4

If there were a Divine Power, all of the world's oil would be under Denmark.   *A friend of Calvin Trillin's*

5

If your prayers were always answered, you'd have reason to doubt the wisdom of God.   *Unknown*

6

If God doesn't destroy Hollywood Boulevard, he owes Sodom and Gomorrah an apology.   *Jay Leno*

7

If God is a Catholic, how come he only had one son?

Unknown

8

I was raised Catholic and received the body and blood of Christ every Sunday at Communion until the age of thirty, when I became a vegetarian.

Joe Queenan

9

Bart Simpson says Grace:

"Dear God, we paid for all this stuff ourselves, so thanks for nothing."

Matt Groening

1 0

You're born. You suffer. You die. Fortunately, there's a loophole.

Billy Graham

1 1

The atheists have produced a Christmas play. It's called *Coincidence on 34th Street*.

Jay Leno

12
Jesus loves you, but everybody else thinks you're a jerk.
Unknown

13

Evil dwells in moist places.

Sister Mary Olivia

14

Lord, give me patience . . . and hurry!

George Robinson Ragsdale

15

Two great European narcotics are alcohol and Christianity.

Friedrich Nietzsche (1844–1900)

Nietzsche was stupid and abnormal.

Leo Tolstoy (1828–1910)

16

God is dead.

Friedrich Nietzsche, in 1882

Nietzsche is dead.

God, in 1900

Jason Lioi

17

Humankind can't stand too much reality.

T. S. Eliot (1888–1965)

18

Reality is that which, when you stop believing in it, doesn't go away.   *Philip K. Dick*

19

Reality is something you rise above.

Liza Minnelli

20

Reality is the leading cause of stress for those in touch with it.   *Jane Wagner*

21

Idealism is fine, but as it approaches reality the cost becomes prohibitive.   *William F. Buckley*

22

Reality is a temporary illusion brought on by an absence of beer.   *Unknown*

23

Life is full of misery, loneliness, and suffering—and it's all over much too soon.   *Woody Allen*

24

This life is a test; it is only a test. If it were a real life, you would receive instructions on where to go and what to do.

Unknown

25

The purpose of life is to fight maturity.

Dick Werthimer

26

Life is a moderately good play with a badly written third act.

Truman Capote (1924–1984)

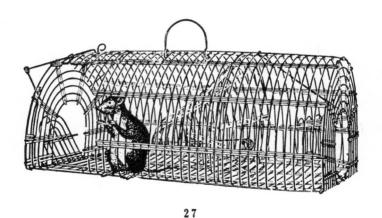

27

All the world's a cage.

Jeanne Phillips

28

How is it possible to find meaning in a finite world, given my waist and shirt size?   *Woody Allen*

29

There are two reasons why the world is so screwed up: men and women.   *Unknown*

30

Not only is life a bitch, it has puppies.

Adrienne E. Gusoff

31

The more crap you believe, the better off you are.

Charles Bukowski

32

I think, therefore I'm single.

Liz Winston

33

I don't think of myself as single. I'm romantically challenged.   *Stephanie H. Piro*

34

I have often depended on the blindness of strangers.
Adrienne E. Gusoff

35

Opportunity knocked. My doorman threw him out.
Adrienne E. Gusoff

36

When I'm in a wig, i'm pretty attractive. I stare at mirrors
because I'm my type.   *Kevin McDonald*

37

Bookstore pickup line:
   "Have you seen a copy of *Tax Tips For Billionaires*?"
David Letterman

38

To attract men I wear a perfume called "New Car Inte-
rior."   *Rita Rudner*

39

A man on a date wonders if he'll get lucky. The woman
already knows.   *Monica Piper*

40

What is my favorite romantic spot? You mean in the whole world or on somebody's body?

Jackie Mason

41

If you want to say it with flowers, remember that a single rose screams in your face: "I'm cheap!"

Delta Burke

42

You can say it with flowers
You can say it with wine
But to make her stinkin' sentimental,
Say it with a Lincoln Continental.

Robert Byrne

Robert Byrne should be gagged.

Tracy Chreene

43

My girlfriend says I never listen to her. I think that's what she said. *Drake Sather*

44

The man who waits for the woman to make the first move
is the man of his dreams. *Robert Byrne*

45

Never sign a valentine with your own name.
Charles Dickens (1812–1870)

4 6

His voice was as intimate as the rustle of sheets.
Dorothy Parker (1893–1967)

4 7

I thought I told you to wait in the car.
*Tallulah Bankhead (1903–1968) on seeing
a former lover for the first time in years.*

4 8

The one who loves the least controls the relationship.
Robert Anthony

4 9

Love is the only disease that makes you feel better.
Sam Shepard

5 0

To fall in love you have to be in the state of mind for it to
take, like a disease.
Nancy Mitford (1904–1973)

5 1

I'd rather be in jail than in love again.

from the 1991 movie Hear My Song

5 2

I fall in love with any girl who smells of library paste.

from Peanuts, *by Charles Schulz*

5 3

No matter how lovesick a woman is, she shouldn't take the first pill that comes along.

Dr. Joyce Brothers

5 4

Before I met my husband, I'd never fallen in love, though I'd stepped in it a few times. *Rita Rudner*

5 5

In love with her own husband? Monstrous! What a selfish woman! *Jennie Jerome Churchill (1854–1921)*

5 6

Falling out of love is very enlightening. For a short while you see the world with new eyes. *Iris Murdoch*

5 7

I've had only three wives and three guitars in my life, though I've flirted with others.

Andrés Segovia (1893–1987)

5 8

Platonic love is being invited into the wine cellar for a sip of pop.   *Unknown*

5 9

Sex between a man and a woman can be wonderful— provided you get between the right man and woman.

Woody Allen

60

Nobody loves me like my mother, and she could be jivin', too.

B. B. King

61

I believe that sex is the most beautiful, natural, and wholesome thing that money can buy.

Steve Martin

62

Never lie down with a woman who's got more troubles than you.

Nelson Algren (1909–1981)

63

If God had meant us to have group sex, he'd have given us more organs.

Malcolm Bradbury

64

Mistresses and wives are as different as night and day.

Abigail Van Buren

65

Shopping is better than sex. If you're not satisfied after shopping, you can make an exchange for something you *really* like.   *Adrienne E. Gusoff*

66

I tried phone sex and it gave me an ear infection.
                                          Richard Lewis

67

I was pretty old before I had my first sexual experience. The reason was that I was born by Caesarian section and had no frame of reference.   *Jeff Hilton*

68

Coito, ergo sum.

Unknown

69

I slept with a French girl once. It wasn't magical, it wasn't mystical, and it wasn't worth five bucks.

Tony Morewood

70

When the sun comes up, I have morals again.

Elayne Boosler

71

Why do they put the Gideon Bibles only in the bedrooms, where it's usually too late?

Christopher Darlington Morley (1890–1957)

72

Never trust a husband too far or a bachelor too near.

Helen Rowland (1876–1950)

Puritans should wear fig leaves on their eyes.

Stanislaw J. Lec

Sexual congress in a Mailer novel is always a matter of strenuous endeavor, rather like mountain climbing.

Kate Millet

Kate Millet is an imploding beanbag of poisonous self-pity.

Camille Paglia

Camille Paglia is a crassly egocentric, raving twit.

Molly Ivins

A 400-ft. diaphragm! Birth control for the whole country at once!

Woody Allen

When my mom found my diaphragm, I told her it was a bathing cap for my cat.

Liz Winston

78

I rely on my personality for birth control.

Liz Winston

79

Sometimes I look at a cute guy and get a uterus twinge.

Carrie Snow

80

A hooker told me she'd do anything I wanted for fifty bucks. I said, "Paint my house."

Henny Youngman

81

When they said "Make love, not war" at Woodstock, they never imagined that one would become as dangerous as the other.

Jay Leno

82

Today when you get the clap, it's a relief.

Brad Garrett

8 3

I finally found my wife's G spot. A neighbor lady had it.
Jim Sherbert

84

Why do Kennedy men cry during sex?
Mace.   *Unknown*

85

I wrote the story myself. It's about a girl who lost her
reputation and never missed it.

Mae West (1892–1980)

86

I married a German. Every night I dress up as Poland and
he invades me.   *Bette Midler*

87

Intercourse counterfeits masturbation.

Jean-Paul Sartre (1905–1980)

88

If Moses had seen her first, we wouldn't have the Sixth
Commandment.   *Unknown*

89

Masturbation is the thinking man's television.

Christopher Hampton

90

If you can't stand the heat, stay out of the bedroom.
David E. Ortman

91

The biggest, strongest, most powerful men can be reduced by sex to imps.
Isaac Bashevis Singer (1904–1991)

92

Yuppies have a low birth rate because they have to go to Aspen to mate.   *Dave Barry*

93

Incest is relatively boring.

Unknown

94

Being a sex symbol was rather like being a convict.   *Raquel Welch*

95

Chastity is its own punishment.

James H. Pou Bailey

96

When she saw the "Members Only" sign she thought of him.   *Spike Milligan*

97

What the world needs is fewer people making more people.   *George Burns*

We all worry about the population explosion, but not at the right time.
Arthur Hoppe

99

A paddlewheel river boat is as beautiful as a wedding cake, without the complications.
Mark Twain (1835–1910)

100

Just because I have rice in my clothes doesn't mean I've been to a wedding. A Chinese person threw up on me.
Phyllis Diller

101

At weddings, one family is always better than the other.
Jeff Foxworthy

102

My husband and I didn't sign a prenuptial agreement. We signed a mutual suicide pact.

Roseanne Barr Arnold

103

Roseanne Barr is a bowling ball looking for an alley.

Mr. Blackwell

104

Marriage is for those who have given up the struggle.

Quentin Crisp

105

If marriage is the most natural state, how come married people always look nauseous?   *Jackie Mason*

106

A wholesome sexual relationship changes with marriage because all of a sudden you're sleeping with a relative.

Andrew Ward

107

My husband is two years younger than he thinks I am.

Rita Rudner

108

Married men live longer than single men, but they suffer a slow, tortured death.   *Larry Reeb*

109

When you marry your mistress, you create a job vacancy.

James Goldsmith

110

A fool and his money are soon married.

Variously ascribed

111

Being married reduces the chance of a heart attack, or anything exciting.

Jonathan Katz

112

Marriage is a strange relationship. It's very hard to live in the same house with someone all the time if you're a grown-up person. *Katharine Hepburn*

113

In some countries, marriage is used as a punishment for shoplifting.

from the 1992 movie Wayne's World

114

If you hate solitude, avoid marriage.

Anton Chekhov (1860–1904)

115

After 27 years of marriage, my wife and I have finally achieved sexual compatibility. Now we get simultaneous headaches. *Clifford Kuhn*

116

A girl can't analyze marriage, and a woman dare not.

Lady Troubridge (1902–1946)

117

Most men who are not married by the age of thirty-five are either homosexual or smart.

Becky Rodenbeck

118

Both of my ex-wives closed their eyes when making love because they didn't want to see me having a good time.

Joseph Wambaugh

119

Your spouse should be just attractive enough to turn you on. Anything more is trouble.

Albert Brooks

120

Marriage is the only adventure open to the cowardly.

Voltaire (1694–1778)

121

I told my mother-in-law that my house was her house, and she said, "Get the hell off my property."

Joan Rivers

1 2 2

Marriage starts with passion and ends with laundry.
Michael J. Hogan

1 2 3

My mother buried three husbands, and two of them were just napping. *Rita Rudner*

1 2 4

I never heard of a trial separation that didn't work.
Lawrence Block

125

My marriage didn't work out. I was a human being and he was a Klingon.   *Carol Liefer*

126

If I had murdered my wife on our wedding day fifteen years ago, I would have gotten less time than that.

Frank Atkinson

127

I don't believe in divorce. I believe in widowhood.

Carolyn Green

128

Marriage is a souvenir of love.

Helen Rowland (1876–1950)

129

I never got married because I couldn't see bringing a partner in for my money.

Jackie Mason, who got married in 1991

I've never been married, but I tell people I'm divorced so they won't think something's wrong with me.

Elayne Boosler

131

Drunkenness is voluntary insanity.

Seneca (4 B.C.–A.D. 65)

132

I was so drunk last night I fell down and missed the floor.

Harry Crane for Dean Martin

133

If you drink like a fish, swim, don't drive.

Bumper sticker

134

When I read about the evils of drinking, I gave up reading.

Henny Youngman

135

There are more old drunkards than old doctors.

Proverb

136

A man should be upright, not kept upright.

Marcus Aurelius (121–180)

137

I envy people who drink. At least they have something to blame everything on.

Oscar Levant (1906–1972)

138

There's nothing wrong with Oscar Levant that a miracle wouldn't cure.

Alexander Woollcott (1887–1943)

139

Giving birth is like pushing a flaming log through your nostril.

Unknown

140

Giving birth is like taking your lower lip and forcing it over your head.

Carol Burnett

141

I was so ugly when I was born the doctor slapped everybody. *Jim Bailey as Phyllis Diller*

142

My mother groan'd, my father wept,
Into the dangerous world I leapt.
William Blake (1757–1827)

143

I was born because my mother needed a fourth at meals.
Beatrice Lillie (1898–1989)

144

My wife was in labor for thirty-two hours and I was faith-
ful to her the whole time. *Jonathan Katz*

145

When I was a kid I once stole a pornographic book in
braille and rubbed the dirty parts.
Woody Allen

146

When I was little, my mother said to me: "Kennedy has just been assassinated. Go clean your room."

Richard Lewis

147

The imaginary friends I had as a kid dropped me because their friends thought I didn't exist.

Aaron Machado

148

Before I had kids I went home after work to rest. Now I go to work to rest.   *Simon Ruddell*

149

Children are all foreigners.

Ralph Waldo Emerson (1803–1882)

150

The secret of eternal youth is arrested development.

Alice Roosevelt Longworth (1884–1980)

151

There is nothing so aggravating as a boy who is too old to ignore and too young to kick.

Elbert Hubbard (1856–1915)

152

Youth is a disease that must be borne patiently. Time will cure it. *R. H. Benson (1871–1914)*

153

Mothers are a biological necessity; fathers are a social invention. *Margaret Mead (1901–1978)*

154

The reason for the success of *Clan of the Cave Bear* is that it's about a Cro-Magnon child being raised by a family of Neanderthals—a position almost all of us have been in. *Lawrence Block*

155

If your parents never had children, chances are you won't, either. *Dick Cavett*

156

My wife wanted to call our daughter Sue, but I felt that in our family that was usually a verb.

Dennis Wolfberg

157

The goodness of a pun is proportional to its intolerableness. *Edgar Allan Poe (1809–1849)*

Three-fifths of Edgar Allan Poe is genius and two-fifths sheer fudge. *James Russell Lowell (1819–1891)*

158

No man is responsible for his father. That is entirely his mother's affair.   *Margaret Turnbull (1920–1942)*

159

My mother used to say that there are no strangers, only friends you haven't yet met. She's now in a maximum security twilight home in Australia.

Dame Edna Everage

160

There are three ways to get something done—do it yourself, hire someone to do it, or ask your kids not to do it.

Malcolm Kushner

161

My kid beat up your honor student.

Bumper sticker

162

My parents keep asking why I never come home for a visit. It's because Delta Airlines won't wait in the yard while I run in.   *Margaret Smith*

163

The sins of the fathers are often visited upon the sons-in-law.
John Kiser

164

School is where you go between when your parents can't take you and industry can't take you.

John Updike

165

What are schools for if not indoctrination against Communism?
Richard Nixon

166

Education is the ability to listen to almost anything without losing your temper.

Robert Frost (1874–1963)

167

If men liked shopping, they'd call it research.

Cynthia Nelms

The same time that women came up with PMS, men came up with ESPN. *Blake Clark*

Give a man a fish and he eats for a day. Teach him how to fish and you get rid of him for the whole weekend.

Zenna Schaffer

170

There should be PMS shelters for men.

Jeff Foxworthy

171

Behind every successful man is a surprised woman.

Maryon Pearson (1901–1989)

172

Since, as you say, Geoffrey, we only pass this way but once, it seems a shame to be such a pompous ass.

Cartoon caption by Stevenson

173

I like the concept of "men." It's the reality I have trouble with.

Stephanie H. Piro

174

The difference between government bonds and men is that government bonds mature.

Debbie Perry

175

I'm not bald, I'm a person of scalp.

Unknown

176

I'm not really bald. I'm a hair donor.

Clifford Kuhn

177

The most delightful advantage of being bald is that you can hear snowflakes. *R. G. Daniels*

178

Men with hair in the daytime are overdressed.

Joe Garagiola

179

Ever have one of those nights when you didn't want to go out but your hair looked too good to stay home?

Jack Simmons

180

A good woman is one of the greatest things on earth,
second only perhaps to a good child or a good man.

Stephen Leacock (1869–1944)

181

If a woman hasn't met the right man by the time she's 24,
she may be lucky. *Deborah Kerr*

182

I would venture to guess that Anon, who wrote so many poems without signing them, was a woman.

Virginia Woolf (1882–1941)

183

Roosters crow, hens deliver.

Feminist slogan

184

My wife has never suffered from stress, but she's a carrier.

Blake Clark

185

Beauty is in the eye of the cuckholder.

Robert Byrne

Robert Byrne should be gagged.

Tracy Chreene

186

If women were as big as men, we'd be in real trouble.

Terry McDonald

187

If a woman's work is never done, she should start earlier.

Ron Stevens

188

Why dust the house when you can just wait a couple of years and get a snowblower?   *Unknown*

189

The way to fight a woman is with your hat—grab it and run.   *John Barrymore (1882–1942)*

190

She laughs at everything you say. Why? Because she has fine teeth.   *Benjamin Franklin (1706–1790)*

191

One cannot be always laughing at a man without now and then stumbling on something witty.

Jane Austen (1775–1817)

192

Women who buy perfume and flowers for themselves because men don't do it are "self basting."

Adair Lara

193

Housework can't kill you, but why take a chance?

Phyllis Diller

194

Housekeeping ain't no joke.

Louisa May Alcott (1832–1888)

195

The classic function of the "warrior" helped men throughout history achieve a sense of confidence they needed in order to cope with women.

Page Smith

196

When women are depressed they either eat or go shopping. Men invade another country. It's a whole different way of thinking. *Elayne Boosler*

197

Men differ from women. You never see young men sitting around talking about their dream weddings.

Charles Cosart

198

When the trust goes out of a relationship, it's no fun lying anymore.

from "Cheers"

199

The difference between men and women is that a man can walk past a shoe store, especially if he already has a pair of shoes.

Gallagher

200

You're sexy when you're sick.
(One of the 17,687 things men say that aggravate women.)

Robert Byrne

201

I come from a family where gravy is considered a beverage.

Erma Bombeck

202

If you don't show up at a party, people will assume you're fat.
from "Newhart"

203

Cooking is like love. It should be entered into with abandon or not at all.
Harriet Van Horne

204

The guy who invented headcheese must have been really hungry.
Jerry Seinfeld

205

My husband thinks that health food is anything he eats before the expiration date.
Rita Rudner

206

Bulimics make me sick.

Joe Vecchio

207

What you eat standing up doesn't count.

Beth Barnes

208

Food is an important part of a balanced diet.

Fran Lebowitz

209

I was a vegetarian until I started leaning toward the sunlight.

Rita Rudner

210

Diner: "What's the specialty of the house?"
Waitress: "The Heimlich Maneuver."

Cartoon caption by Meyer

211

I'm on a Valium diet. I take four for breakfast, and the rest of the day the food keeps falling out of my mouth.

Max Alexander

212

There is no politician in India daring enough to explain to the masses that cows can be eaten.

Indira Gandhi (1917–1984)

213

A food is not necessarily essential just because your child
hates it. *Katharine Whitehorn*

214

Revenge is sweet and not fattening.
Alfred Hitchcock (1899–1980)

215

There is something soothing about a pumpkin.
Terry Pimsleur, President,
International Pumpkin Association

216

For women, eating has taken on the sinful status once
reserved for sex. *Unknown*

217

If you don't find our canned corned beef to be all you
hoped it would be, just leave word with the executor of
your estate to return the unopened cans to us for a re-
fund. *Bob and Ray*

218

I am a vegetarian not for my health, but for the health of the chickens.

Isaac Bashevis Singer (1904–1991)

219

My mother is such a lousy cook that Thanksgiving at her house is a time of sorrow.   *Rita Rudner*

220

Cooking tip: Wrap turkey leftovers in aluminum foil and throw them out.   *Nicole Hollander*

221

Health consists of having the same diseases as one's neighbors.   *Quentin Crisp*

222

Preserving health by too severe a rule is a worrisome maladay.   *La Rochefoucauld (1613–1680)*

223

Ever notice that fifteen minutes into a Jerry Lewis telethon you start rooting for the disease?

Jim Sherbert

224

The entire economy of the Western world is built on things that cause cancer.

from the 1985 movie Bliss

225

I want all hellions to quit puffing that hell fume into God's clean air.

Carrie Nation (1846–1911) on smoking

226

Smoking is much more enjoyable around non-smokers.

Dr. Bob Benn

227

Whiskey is the most popular of the remedies that won't cure a cold.

Jerry Vale

228

I told the doctor I broke my leg in two places. He told me to quit going to those places.

Henny Youngman

229

Doctors have identified a new disfiguring disease called the DMV Syndrome. Untreated victims look like their driver's license photos. *from Nick at Night*

230

They certainly give very strange names to diseases.

Plato (427–347 B.C.)

Plato was a bore.

Friedrich Nietzsche (1844–1900)

231

I have flabby thighs, but fortunately my stomach covers them. *Joan Rivers*

232

Walking like a dork is popular among people who used to jog for their health but can no longer afford orthopedic surgery. *Dave Barry*

233

The ultimate indignity is to be given a bedpan by a stranger who calls you by your first name.

Maggie Kuhn

234

One has a greater sense of intellectual degradation after an interview with a doctor than from any human experience.   *Alice James (1848–1892)*

235

Doctors and nurses are people who give you medicine until you die.   *Deborah Martin*

236

I'm sick of hearing about twelve-step programs for healing and recovery. What we need are fewer twelve-step programs and more twelve-gauge shotguns.

Name withheld by request

237

Other people have analysis. I have Utah.

Robert Redford

238

I don't jog. It makes the ice jump right out of my glass.
Martin Mull

239

Middle age is such a nice change from being young.
Dorothy Canfield Fisher

240

Middle age is when a narrow waist and a broad mind begin to change places. *Glenn Dorenbush*

241

My husband will never chase another woman. He's too fine, he's too decent, he's too old.
Gracie Allen (1906–1964) in 1960, when
George Burns was only 64.

242

When the grandmothers of today hear the word "Chippendales," they don't think of chairs.
Joan Kerr

At age 82, I sometimes feel like a twenty-year-old, but there is seldom one around.
Milton Berle

244

The tragedy of an aging woman is that she loses her power over men, often the only power she ever had.

Joyce Power

245

The older one grows, the more one likes indecency.

Virginia Woolf (1882–1941)

246

Be nice to your children, for they will choose your rest home.

Phyllis Diller

247

It's hard to be nostalgic when you can't remember anything.

Unknown

248

No man knows what true happiness is until he has a complete set of false teeth and has lost all interest in the opposite sex.

Lord Rosebery (1847–1929)

249

I'm so old that bartenders check my pulse instead of my
I.D.   *Louise Bowie at 75*

250

I have long thought that the aging process could be
slowed down if it had to work its way through Congress.
                                    George Bush's gag writers

251

Age doesn't matter unless you are a cheese.
                                    Billie Burke (1885–1970)

252

I was going to commit suicide by sticking my head in the
oven, but there was a cake in it.   *Leslie Boone*

253

Always carry a gun. Not to shoot yourself, but to know
that you are always making a choice.
                                    Lina Wertmuller

254

Being a living legend is better than being a dead legend.
George Burns

255

I have never killed a man, but I have read many obituaries
with a lot of pleasure.

Clarence Darrow (1857–1938)

256

Life is pleasant. Death is peaceful. It's the transition that's
troublesome.   *Isaac Asimov (1920–1992)*

257

What I look forward to is continued immaturity followed
by death.   *Dave Barry*

258

I would never die for my beliefs because I might be wrong.
Bertrand Russell (1872–1970)

259

I didn't attend the funeral, but I sent a nice letter saying
I approved of it.   *Mark Twain (1835–1910)*

260

The living are the dead on vacation.

Maurice de Maeterlinck (1862–1949)

261

It's all been rather lovely.

Last words of British actor John Le Mesurier (1912–1983)

262

I have one last request. Don't use embalming fluid on me. I want to be stuffed with crabmeat.

Woody Allen

263

The color of truth is gray.

André Gide (1869–1951)

264

Nobody speaks the truth when there's something they must have.
Elizabeth Bowen (1899–1973)

265

Everybody lies, but it doesn't matter because nobody listens.
Nick Diamos

266

I have convincing proof that I speak the truth: my poverty.
Plato (428–347 B.C.)

Plato was a bore.
Friedrich Nietzsche (1844–1900)

267

Cynicism is an unpleasant way of saying the truth.
Lillian Hellman (1905–1984)

268

Let us begin by committing ourselves to the truth, to find the truth, to speak the truth, and to live with the truth.
Richard Nixon

269

Nixon's motto was, if two wrongs don't make a right, try three.
Norman Cousins (1912–1990)

270

Of all noxious animals, the most noxious is the tourist.
Francis Kilvert (1840–1879)

271

Man is the only animal that fears children.

Sparrow

272

The eagle may soar, but the weasel never gets sucked into a jet engine.

from "Simon and Simon"

273

Cross a termite with a praying mantis and you get a bug that says grace before eating your house.

Unknown

274

Britain plans to stop the breeding of pit bulls. It's hard enough to put a muzzle on a pit bull—lots of luck with those condoms.

Jay Leno

275

If a pit bull romances your leg, fake an orgasm.

Hut Landon

276

My dog is worried about the economy because Alpo is up to 99 cents a can. That's almost $7.00 in dog money.

Joe Weinstein

277

Dog scientists, hoping to make life better for their species, struggle to understand the principle of the doorknob.

Cartoon caption by Gary Larson

278

Dogs are wolves without ideals.

Sparrow

279

Other dogs look at French poodles and wonder if they are members of a weird religious cult.   *Rita Rudner*

280

In my former life I was a sanitary landfill.

Garfield (Jim Davis)

281

Cats are a waste of fur.

Rita Rudner

282

Every life should have nine cats.

Unknown

283

I'm middle of the road. I'd buy a fur coat, but I wouldn't buy a Japanese fur coat.

Cartoon caption by Robert Weber

284

I love animals. I love fur coats. I don't see the connection.

Susan Green

285

My favorite animal is steak.

Fran Lebowitz

Part Two

The Human Condition
Celebrity and Boredom
Music, Art, and Television
Geography and Travel
Sports and Work
Crime, Money, and Lawyers
Business and Government
Politics
Stupidity
War
Jews
Writing and Writers
Books
Questions

286

Stoop and you'll be stepped on; stand tall and you'll be shot at. *Carlos A. Urbizo*

287

A stale mind is the devil's breadbox.

Mary Bly

288

I can think of nothing less pleasurable than a life devoted to pleasure. *John D. Rockefeller (1839–1937)*

289

There is freedom in getting completely screwed up because you know things can't get any worse.
from the 1990 movie The Freshman

290

Living in a vacuum sucks.

Adrienne E. Gusoff

291

It is a common delusion that you make things better by talking about them.

Dame Rose Macaulay (1889–1958)

292

Talking about your troubles is no good. Eighty percent of your friends don't care and the rest are glad.

Tommy Lasorda

293

Blame someone else and get on with your life.

Alan Woods

294

When somebody says, "The last thing I want to do is hurt you," it means that they've got other things to do first.

Mark Schiff

295

Once in a while you have to take a break and visit yourself.

Audrey Giorgi

296

We are inclined to believe those whom we do not know because they have never deceived us.

Samuel Johnson (1709–1784)

There is no arguing with Johnson, for when his pistol misses fire, he knocks you down with the butt.

Oliver Goldsmith (1728–1774)

297

I tend to live in the past because most of my life is there.

Herb Caen

298

Experience is what you get when you don't get what you want.

Unknown

299

We learn from experience that we don't learn from experience.

George Bernard Shaw (1856–1950)

Shaw is too much gas-bag.

D. H. Lawrence (1885–1930)

300

Some days you're a bug, some days you're a windshield.
Price Cobb, after winning a car race in 1988

301

Until you've lost your reputation, you never realize what a burden it was.   *Margaret Mitchell (1909–1949)*

302

Life is a sexually transmitted terminal disease.

Graffito

303

Instant gratification is not soon enough.
from the 1990 movie Postcards from the Edge

304

I feel a lot better since I've given up hope.

Unknown

305

Loneliness is the ultimate poverty.

Abigail Van Buren

306

It makes no difference whether you win or lose until you lose.

Unknown

307

So near and yet so what?

Unknown

308

We forfeit three-fourths of ourselves to be like other people.

Arthur Schopenhauer (1788–1860)

309

Every human being, even if he is an idiot, is a millionaire in emotions.

Isaac Bashevis Singer (1904–1991)

310

People with no vices usually have annoying virtues.

British novelist Elizabeth Taylor

311

Confessions come in pairs.

Sparrow

312

Mother, food, love, and career are the four major guilt groups.
Cathy Guisewite

313

This is the "between you and I" generation.
Eric Severeid

314

A paranoid is someone who knows a little of what's going on.
William Burroughs

315

Clothes aren't dirty unless someone sees you in them.
Logica Paini

316

Anyone with more than 365 pairs of shoes is a pig.
Barbara Melser Lieberman

317

Fashion is something that goes in one year and out the other.
Unknown

318

How many more bathroom-window curtains must die needlessly to clothe golfers? *Mike Lough*

319

If the shoe fits, it's ugly.

Gold's Law

320

Never wear a hat that has more character than you do.

Michael Harris

321

Publicity is like poison. It only hurts you if you swallow it.

Sam Rutigliano

322

I had a terrible nightmare. I dreamed there were eight Gabor sisters. *Unknown*

323

Zsa Zsa Gabor has been married so many times she has rice marks on her face. *Henny Youngman*

324

How many husbands have I had? You mean apart from my own? *Zsa Zsa Gabor*

325

You can calculate Zsa Zsa Gabor's age by the rings on her fingers. *Bob Hope*

326

When Zsa Zsa Gabor went to jail for slapping a cop, the warden put her cellmate on a 24-hour suicide watch.

Jay Leno

327

Arnold Schwarzenegger looks like a condom full of walnuts. *Clive James*

328

An actor is a guy who, if you ain't talking about him, ain't listening. *Marlon Brando*

329

I have the eyes of a dead pig.

Marlon Brando

330

Quitting acting is a sign of maturity.

Marlon Brando

331

Most of the time, Brando sounds like he has a mouth full of wet toilet paper. *Rex Reed*

332

Los Angeles is like a watering hole for mad animals.
British actress Sammi Davis

333

I'm going to stay in show business until I'm the last one left. *George Burns*

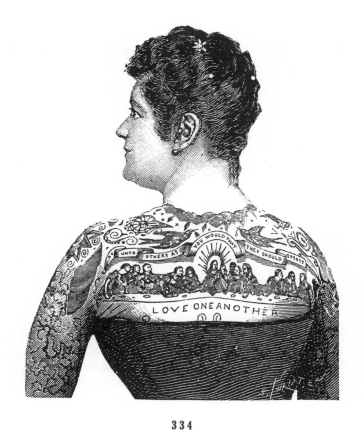

334

My wife and I can put tattoos on our buttocks without fear of negative publicity.

One of Stanley Bing's sixteen reasons he's glad he isn't famous.

335

Shirley MacLaine could go to group therapy all by herself.
Cynthia Nelms

336

I look like a rock quarry that someone has dynamited.
Charles Bronson

337

Jack Benny couldn't ad-lib a belch after a Hungarian dinner.
Fred Allen (1894–1956)

338

Somebody's boring me. I think it's me.
Dylan Thomas (1914–1953)

339

When you're bored with yourself, marry and be bored with someone else.
David Pryce-Jones

340

There is something curiously boring about somebody else's happiness.
Aldous Huxley (1894–1963)

341

I am one of those unhappy persons who inspire bores to the greatest flights of art.

Dame Edith Sitwell (1887–1984)

342

The cello has such a lugubrious sound, like someone reading a will.   *Irene Thomas*

Song Titles

What's Made Milwaukee Famous Has Made a
Loser Out of Me   *Jerry Lee Lewis, 1966*
You're the Reason Our Kids Are Ugly
                    Conway Twitty and Loretta Lynn, 1978
All My Ex's Live in Texas   *George Strait, 1987*
Everytime You Go Outside I Hope It Rains
                              Burch Sisters, 1988
One Day When You Swing That Skillet, My Face
Ain't Gonna Be There.   *John Pate, 1988*
If I Had Knowed You Had Wanted to Went with
Me, I Woulda Seen You Had Got to Get to Go.
                              Fernwood 2-Night
The Bird Nest Out My Window Is the Wig You
Used to Wear   *Charles Zuppards, 1990*

Politically Correct Songs

Three Visually Challenged Mice
Why Can't a Person Be More Like a Person?
African American Is the Color of My True Love's
Hair
My Person Sal   *I. C. Dragon*

I compose as a sow piddles.
          Wolfgang Amadeus Mozart (1756–1791)

346

Brass bands are all very well in their place—outdoors and several miles away.

Sir Thomas Beecham (1879–1961)

347

Welcome to hell. Here's your accordian.

Cartoon caption by Gary Larson

348

The reason there are so many Jewish violinists is that our fingers are circumcised, which gives us very good dexterity.

Itzak Perlman

349

Accordians don't play "Lady of Spain," people do.

Herb Caen

350

I played first chair in the high school band until they gave me an instrument. *George R. Hext*

351

When buying a used car, punch the buttons on the radio.
If all the stations are rock and roll, there's a good chance
that the transmission is shot.   *Larry Lujack*

352

The chief objection of playing a wind instrument is that it
prolongs the life of the player.

George Bernard Shaw (1856–1950)

353

I wish the government would put a tax on pianos for the incompetent. *Dame Edith Sitwell (1887–1984)*

354

My musical talent is less God-given than taketh away.
Steve Rubenstein

355

Blood should be stirred before it's spilled, and nothing does it better than bagpipes. *Ervin Lewis*

356

Michelangelo was a pornographer.

Camille Paglia

Get this woman a Valium! Hand her a gin. Camille, honey, calm down!
Molly Ivins

357

Van Gogh became a painter because he had no ear for music.
Nikki Harris

358

A portrait is a picture in which there is something wrong with the mouth.
Eugene Speicher (1883–1962)

359

See what will happen if you don't stop biting your finger-nails?

Will Rogers (1879–1935), to his niece on seeing the Venus de Milo.

360

If you couldn't read, you couldn't look up what was on television.
from "Leave It to Beaver"

361

The great thing about television is that if something important happens anywhere in the world, day or night, you can always change the channel. *from "Taxi"*

362

Television is a medium of entertainment that permits millions of people to listen to the same joke at the same time and yet remain lonesome.

T. S. Eliot (1888–1965)

363

I'm pleased that television is now showing murder stories, because it brings murder back into its rightful setting—the home. *Alfred Hitchcock (1889–1980)*

364

If it weren't for electricity, we'd all be watching television by candlelight. *George Gobel (1920–1991)*

365

You should climb Mount Fujiyama once in your life. Climb it twice and you're a fool. *Japanese saying*

366

Europe is so rich in history that sometimes you can barely stand it.   *Dave Barry*

367

The worst thing about Europe is that you can't go out in the middle of the night and get a Slurpee.

Tellis Frank

368

Why was I born Scandinavian? The food is bad, the weather is terrible, and the theology can break a man's heart.   *Garrison Keillor*

369

Hell is a city much like London.

Percy Bysshe Shelley (1792–1822)

Rome makes me think of a man who keeps himself by showing visitors the corpse of his grandmother.

James Joyce (1882–1941)

[James Joyce is] nothing but old fags and cabbage-stumps of quotations from the Bible and the rest, stewed in the juice of deliberate, journalistic dirty-mindedness.

D. H. Lawrence (1885–1930)

London, though handsomer than Paris, is not so handsome as Philadelphia.

Thomas Jefferson (1743–1826)

American life is a powerful solvent.

George Santayana (1863–1952)

What a pity, when Christopher Columbus discovered America, that he ever mentioned it.

Margot Asquith (1864–1945)

374

I moved to New York City for my health. I'm paranoid and it was the only place where my fears were justified.

Anita Weiss

375

New York is the only city in the world where you can be awakened by a smell.

Jeff Garland

376

In New York City, one suicide in ten is attributed to a shortage of storage space.

Judith Stone

377

I like New York because I get paid three hours earlier.

Henny Youngman

378

In Miami, there are rallies for the right to sacrifice chickens.

Dave Barry

379

In Greenville, South Carolina, I once saw a guy autographing books he had read.

Jack Simmons

380

California gave the nation Richard Nixon and Ronald Reagan. May its grapes rot.   *Mike Royko*

381

In California schools, Chief Crazy Horse is called either Chief Sitting Dude or Chief Mentally Impaired Horse because the word "crazy" might offend those who are out of their minds.   *Joe Queenan*

382

It's redundant to die in Los Angeles.
Truman Capote (1924–1984)

383

Moving from Los Angeles to Petaluma is the best thing I ever did. I like having neighbors who haven't written screenplays.   *Rick Reynolds*

384

Great God! This is an awful place!
Captain Robert Falcon Scott (1870–1912), on
arriving at the South Pole.

385

Home is where you hang your head.

Unknown

386

The two best things about traveling are arriving in a new city and leaving it.

Unknown

387

I have paid as much as $300 a night to throw up into a sink shaped like a seashell.

Erma Bombeck

388

Once you see the drivers in Indonesia you understand why religion plays such a big part in their lives.

Erma Bombeck

389

Too often travel, instead of broadening the mind, merely lengthens the conversation.

Elizabeth Drew (1887–1965)

390

A horseshoe can't bring good luck because every horse in the race carries four.   *Red Smith (1905–1982)*

391

Attention! The train arriving at platforms eight, nine, ten, and eleven is arriving sideways.   *Unknown*

392

The first time I walked into a trophy shop, I looked around and thought to myself, "This guy is *good*!"

Fred Wolf

393

To be a good pitcher you need strong legs and a big butt.

Nolan Ryan

394

I quit coaching because of illness and fatigue. The fans were sick and tired of me.   *John Ralston*

395

Nobody in the game of football should be called a genius. A genius is somebody like Norman Einstein.

Former quarterback Joe Theisman

396
Women don't box because they don't want to weigh in.
Unknown

397
Anybody who watches three games of football in a row
should be declared brain dead.

Erma Bombeck

398

When you've got the football and eleven guys are chasing you, and you're smart, you run. It was no big deal.
Red "The Galloping Ghost" Grange in 1991

399

Football combines the two worst things about American life. It is violence punctuated by committee meetings.
George Will

400

Do you have any problems, other than that you're unemployed, a moron, and a dork?

John McEnroe to a fan

401

No man guilty of golf should be eligible for any office of trust or profit in the United States, and all female golfers should be shipped to the white-slave corrals of the Argentine.
H. L. Mencken (1880–1956)

402

When I coached at Niagara, we gave recruits a piece of caramel candy. If they took the wrapper off before eating it, they got a basketball scholarship; otherwise, they got a football scholarship.
Frank Leyden

403

Chess is as elaborate a waste of human intelligence as you can find outside an advertising agency.

Raymond Chandler (1888–1959)

404

All paid jobs absorb and degrade the mind.

Aristotle (384–322 B.C.)

405

Aristotle could have avoided the mistake of thinking that women have fewer teeth than men by the simple device of asking Mrs. Aristotle to open her mouth.

Bertrand Russell (1872–1970)

4 0 6

There is something wrong with my eyesight. I can't see going to work. *Teddy Bergeron*

4 0 7

I had a boring office job. I cleaned the windows in the envelopes. *Rita Rudner*

4 0 8

Opportunities are usually disguised as hard work, so most people don't recognize them.

Ann Landers

4 0 9

Never hire an electrician whose eyebrows are scorched. *Mason Wilder*

4 1 0

To reduce the chances of crime in your home, put a dead-bolt in your door, put a peephole in your door, and move your door to Fresno, California.

Malcolm Kushner

411

The reason there is so little crime in Germany is that it's against the law. *Alex Levin*

412

A man who has never gone to school may steal from a freight car, but if he has a university education he may steal the whole railroad.
Franklin D. Roosevelt (1903–1966)

Roosevelt was one-third Eleanor and two-thirds mush.
Dorothy Parker (1893–1967)

413

A lawyer with a briefcase can steal more than a thousand men with guns. *Mario Puzo*

414

Don't worry about people stealing your ideas. If your ideas are any good, you'll have to ram them down people's throats. *Howard Aiken*

415

There's no satisfaction in hanging a man who does not object to it. *George Bernard Shaw (1856–1950)*

416

We live in an age when pizza gets to your home before the police.

Jeff Marder

417

More university graduates become criminals every year than policemen.

Philip Goodheart

418

The meaning of eternity can't be fully understood until you've heard expert witnesses testify.

Stan Silberg

419

The easiest way for your children to learn about money is for you not to have any.

Katharine Whitehorn

420

If it weren't for baseball, a lot of kids wouldn't even know what a millionaire looks like.

Phyllis Diller

421

My husband is so cheap he won't buy a newspaper. He walks along with the paperboy and asks him questions.

Jim Bailey as Phyllis Diller

422

When it comes to money, everybody is of the same religion.

Voltaire (1694–1778)

423

Lawyers should be buried at sea because deep down they're all right.

Unknown

424

A town that can't support one lawyer can always support two.

American saying

425

There is no shortage of lawyers in Washington, D.C. In fact, there may be more lawyers than people.

Sandra Day O'Connor

Objection!

426

I do not care to speak ill of a man behind his back, but I believe he is an attorney.

Samuel Johnson (1709–1784)

427

The phone company handles 84 billion calls a year—everything from kings, queens, and presidents to the scum of the earth.

Lily Tomlin as Ernestine the Operator

428

Voice mail is the technological upchuck of the age.

Herb Caen

429

I want my data back, scumbag, and I want it back now!
Secretary overheard conversing with her computer

430

In the computer world, hardware is anything you can hit with a hammer, software is what you can only curse at.
Unknown

431

A decision is what a man makes when he can't find anybody to serve on a committee.
Fletcher Knebel

432

There is no monument dedicated to the memory of a committee.
Lester J. Pourciau

433

If we had had more time for discussion, we probably would have made a great many more mistakes.
Leon Trotsky (1879–1940)

If women can sleep their way to the top, how come they aren't there?
Ellen Goodman

An expert is a person who has made all the mistakes that can be made in a very narrow field.

Niels Bohr (1885–1962)

The surest sign that intelligent life exists elsewhere in the universe is that it has never tried to contact us.

Calvin and Hobbes (Bill Watterson)

Astronomy teaches the correct use of the sun and the planets.
Stephen Leacock (1869–1944)

The margin of error in astrology is plus or minus one hundred percent.
Calvin Trillin

439

I've got so far that I could be finished with the whole economic crap in five weeks. . . . This is beginning to bore me.

Karl Marx (1818–1883) while writing Das Kapital

440

Soviet power is a new type of state in which there is no bureaucracy, no police, and no standing army.

Lenin (1870–1924)

441

The people want power, but what on earth would they do with it if it were given to them? *Lenin*

442

He rolled the executions on his tongue like berries.

Osip Mandelstam (1891–1938) on Stalin

443

Communism doesn't work because people like to own stuff. *Frank Zappa*

444

Capitalism, communism . . . it's all garbage.

Msistslav Rostropovich

445

Just because you've been bad at socialism doesn't mean you'll be good at capitalism.   *Michael Thomas*

446

The intermediate stage between socialism and capitalism is alcoholism.   *Norman Brenner*

447

The world would not be in such a snarl
Had Marx been Groucho instead of Karl.

Irving Berlin (1888–1989)

448

Every nation ridicules other nations, and all are right.

Arthur Schopenhauer (1788–1860)

449

I believe that all government is evil, and that trying to improve it is largely a waste of time.

H. L. Mencken (1880–1956)

450

Governments need to have both shepherds and butchers.

Voltaire (1694–1778)

451

The supply of government exceeds the demand.

Lewis Lapham

452

Democracy means people of all races, creeds, and colors working hard so they can afford to move away from people of all races, creeds, and colors.

Johnny Carson

453

Once the people begin to reason, all is lost.

Voltaire (1694–1778)

454

I hate being a bureaucrat and will resign as soon as I know the proper procedure.

Cartoon caption by Hector Breeze

455

I always wanted to get into politics, but I was never light enough to make the team. *Art Buchwald*

456

In order to be the master, the politician poses as the servant. *Charles de Gaulle (1890–1970)*

457

I must follow the people. Am I not their leader?
Benjamin Disraeli (1804–1881)

458

If I return to earth in another life, I hope it's not during a Republican administration. *Timothy Leary*

459

Republicans stand for raw, unbridled evil and greed and ignorance smothered in balloons and ribbons.

Frank Zappa

460

Keep things as they are—Vote for the Sado-Masochist Party.

Unknown

The vote means nothing to women. We should be armed.
Edna O'Brien

462

The reason there are two senators for each state is so that one can be the designated driver.   *Jay Leno*

463

The politicians in Minneapolis are so honest they must be retarded.   *Mike Royko*

464

Somebody has to do something, and it's just incredibly pathetic that it has to be us.

Jerry Garcia of the Grateful Dead

465

What I don't like about politics is that no matter who wins, you lose.   *Alan King*

466

The great thing about democracy is that it gives every voter a chance to do something stupid.

Art Spander

467

If you think Saddam Hussein is a madman, you should meet his brothers Certifiably and Criminally.

Johnny Carson

468

If we don't change direction soon, we'll end up where we're going.   *Professor Irwin Corey*

469

Give me a one-handed economist! All my economists say "On the other hand . . ."

Harry S. Truman (1884–1972)

470

If there had been any formidable body of cannibals in the country, [Franklin Delano Roosevelt] would have promised to provide them with free missionaries fattened at the taxpayer's expense.

H. L. Mencken (1880–1956)

471

Richard Nixon inherited some good instincts from his Quaker forebears, but by diligent hard work he overcame them.   *James Reston*

472

It's nice to be here in Iowa.

Gerald Ford in Ohio, 1976

473

The nuclear button was at one stage at the disposal of a man, Gerald Ford, who might have either pressed it by mistake or else pressed it deliberately to obtain room service. *Clive James*

474

The youthful sparkle in Ronald Reagan's eyes is caused by his contact lenses, which he keeps highly polished.

Sheilah Graham

475

Ronald Reagan: Most of His Polyps Were Benign.

1984 campaign slogan suggested by Dave Barry

476

Lincoln freed the slaves; Bush frays the sleeves.

Graffito

477

George Bush is anti-abortion and pro capital punishment. With him it's just a matter of timing.

Dennis Miller

478

I think George Bush belongs to Jehovah's Bystanders. When his plane went down in World War II, his whole life flashed before him, and he wasn't in it.

Mort Sahl

479

If the answer is "Jerry Brown," the question must be very strange. *Patrick A. Lewis*

480

Democracy means that anyone can grow up to be president, and anyone who doesn't grow up can be vice president. *Johnny Carson*

481

George Bush will lead us out of this recovery.

Dan Quayle

482

Bill Clinton's foreign policy experience stems mainly from having breakfast at The International House of Pancakes.

Pat Buchanan

483

Power failure in Little Rock! Hillary, Tipper, Bill and Al all turned on their blow dryers at the same time!

from the TV show "Murphy Brown"

484

I may be a dumb blonde, but I'm not that blonde.

Patricia Neill

485

Of those who say nothing, few are silent.

Thomas Neill

486

English was good enough for Jesus Christ and it's good enough for the children of Texas.

Texas Governor Miriam "Ma" Ferguson in 1924

487

There's a television commercial where a customer in a drugstore has never heard of Preparation H. Where has he had his head?   *Gallagher*

488

Never attribute to malice what can be adequately explained by stupidity.   *Nick Diamos*

489

During World War II, it was legal to kill a German, but kill one now and all hell breaks loose.

Fred Willard

490

War is a cowardly escape from the problems of peace.
Thomas Mann (1875–1955)

491

War is a brain-spattering, windpipe-splitting art.
Lord Byron (1788–1824)

War is not nice.

Barbara Bush

492

You may not be interested in war, but war is interested in you.
Leon Trotsky (1879–1940)

493

Why does the Air Force need expensive new bombers? Have the people we've been bombing over the years been complaining?
George Wallace

494

It is good to kill an Admiral from time to time to encourage the others.
Voltaire (1694–1778)

495

You can't shake hands with a clenched fist.

Indira Gandhi (1917–1984)

496

Now that the world is wracked by peace, people can go back to what they love best: anti-Semitism.

Mort Sahl

497

When I moved to Los Angeles, I settled in a predominantly anxious neighborhood. Weekends I'd go up the coast to a retreat called Wounded Jew.   *Richard Lewis*

498

My mother has a Jewish satellite dish. It picks up problems from other families.   *Richard Lewis*

499

Jews can't serve on juries because they insist they're guilty.   *Cathy Ladman*

500

Jews don't go camping. Life is hard enough already.

Carol Siskind

501

"Oy to the World"

Jewish Christmas Carol

502

Yo.

Lament from a dyslexic Jew

503

Why do Jewish husbands die before their wives? They want to.

Henny Youngman

504

Jews don't drink much because it interferes with their suffering.

Milton Berle

505

To my grandfather, gentiles were people who sold their children for whiskey.

David Steinberg

506

How odd
Of God
To choose
The Jews.

Ascribed to Hilaire Belloc (1870–1953) and others

Hilaire Belloc is conscious of being decrepit and forgetful, but not of being a bore.

Evelyn Waugh (1903–1966)

507

An author is a fool who, not content with boring those he lives with, insists on boring future generations.

Charles de Montesquieu (1869–1755)

508

When one has no particular talent for anything, one takes to the pen.

Honoré de Balzac (1799–1850)

509

Writers should write about what they don't know about what they know.

Ken Kesey

510

Writing is like driving at night in the fog. You can only see as far as your headlights, but you can make the whole trip that way.
E. L. Doctorow

511

Writing only leads to more writing.

Colette (1873–1954)

Let me tell you about writing for films. You finish your book, you drive to the California border, and you pitch it over. No, on second thought, you first let them toss the money over.   *Ernest Hemingway (1899–1961)*

Hemingway was a jerk.

Harold Robbins

Harold Robbins doesn't sound like an author, he sounds like a company brochure.   *The New Yorker*

For a lesbian bastard writer mental case, I'm doing awfully well.   *Jill Johnston*

A figure of speech can often get into a crack too small for logic.   *Unknown*

The difference between the right word and the almost right word is the difference between lightning and a lightning bug.   *Mark Twain (1835–1910)*

516

If Shakespeare had had to go on an author tour to promote *Romeo and Juliet,* he never would have written *Macbeth.*   *Dr. Joyce Brothers*

517

I have tried lately to read Shakespeare, and found it so intolerably dull that it nauseated me.

Charles Darwin (1809–1882)

518

I have suffered more ghastly evenings with Shakespeare than with any other dramatist.   *Peter Brook*

519

William Shakespeare sounds to me like some kind of faggot.   *Gene Simmons of Kiss*

520

It would positively be a relief to me to dig [Shakespeare] up and throw stones at him.

George Bernard Shaw (1856–1950)

521

When you were quite a little boy, somebody ought to have said "hush" just once.

Mrs. Patrick Campbell (1865–1940) to George Bernard Shaw

522

The way Shaw believes in himself is very refreshing in these atheistic days when so many people believe in no God at all.

Israel Zangwill (1864–1926)

523

I remember coming across [Shaw] at the Grand Canyon and finding him peevish, refusing to admire it or even look at it properly. He was jealous of it.

J. B. Priestley (1894–1984)

524

Shaw writes like a Pakistani who has learned English when he was twelve years old in order to become an accountant.

John Osborne

Well said; that was laid on with a trowel.

William Shakespeare (1564–1616), in As You Like It, *I:2*

525

I've been in love three hundred times in my life, and all but five were with books. *Lee Glickstein*

526

The oldest books are only just out to those who haven't read them. *Samuel Butler (1835–1902)*

527

If you can explain how to write a book, then you don't know how to write one. If you can write a book, then you won't be able to explain how you did it.

Joe Bob Briggs

528

Books That Should Never Get Published
> A Special Kind of Beauty: Nude Studies of Game Show Hosts
> 1,001 Amish Zingers and Put-downs
> Dan Quayle's Big Book of Things You Can Make with Paper Clips

David Letterman and his writers

529

God forbid that any book should be banned. The practice is as indefensible as infanticide.

Rebecca West (1892–1983)

530

Now that I'm trying to sell a book, I'm adorable.

Katharine Hepburn

531

It was a book to kill time for those who like it better dead.

Dame Rose Macaulay (1889–1958)

532

Books are a load of crap.

Philip Larkin (1922–1985)

533

The tears of strangers are only water.

Russian Proverb

534

For every back there is a knife.

Corporate proverb

535

Every bull has a bear behind.

Wall Street proverb

536

Spilled wine is a sign of happiness, but break the bed and all will have long faces.   *Spanish proverb*

537

"Excuse me, did you say something?"
A good reply to the question: "Do you think I'm boring?"
Dick Cavalli

538

"Subordinate Clauses."
Answer to the question: "What do you call Santa's helpers?"   *Dan Wiles*

539

"Feces."
Correct answer to the question, "What's your sign?"

"Seventeen."
Suggested answer to the question: "How many times have
I told you not to spit in the sink?"

"You mean now?"
Possible answer to the question: "What time is it?"

"Why, is one missing?"
Reply to such questions as "Did you take a taxi?
Did you take a shower?"

Early Martin and Lewis

"What game?"
What to reply when asked, "Do you think I take the game
too seriously?"   *Charles M. Schulz*

"Some."

Willie McCovey on being asked on the phone:
"Did I wake you?"

Part Three

Assorted Nuggets

545

The only difference between a rut and a grave is the depth.
Old saying

546

Conscience is a mother-in-law whose visit never ends.
H. L. Mencken (1880–1956)

547

Most saints live to regret their career choice.
Bob Stokes

548

My motto is the same as my blood type: B Positive.
Cynthia Nelms

549

If you are all wrapped up in yourself you are overdressed.
Kate Halvorson

550

The ability to delude yourself may be an important survival tool.
Jane Wagner

551

We are so vain that we even care for the opinion of those we don't care for.

Marie Ebner von Eschenbach (1830–1916)

552

Historians are like deaf people who go on answering questions that no one has asked them.

Leo Tolstoy (1828–1910)

553

A good listener is a good talker with a sore throat.

Katharine Whitehorn

554

People ask for criticism, but they only want praise.

Somerset Maugham (1874–1965)

555

I was going to have cosmetic surgery until I noticed that the doctor's office was full of portraits by Picasso.

Rita Rudner

556

Delusions of grandeur make me feel a lot better about myself.

Jane Wagner

557

I was born with a priceless gift, the ability to laugh at the misfortunes of others.

Dame Edna Everage

558

They laughed at Joan of Arc, but she went right ahead and built it.

Gracie Allen (1906–1964)

559

You might be a redneck if:

1. You think your family reunion is a good place to meet women;
2. Your front porch collapses and kills more than three dogs;
3. Your wife's hairdo was ever destroyed by a ceiling fan;
4. The grass under your refrigerator has turned yellow;
5. You think God looks like Hank Williams, Jr.;
6. You refer to fifth grade as "My senior year."

Jeff Foxworthy

560

Why are we honoring this man? Have we run out of human beings?   *Milton Berle at a Howard Cosell roast*

561

If one sticks too rigidly to one's principles, one would hardly see anybody.

Agatha Christie (1891–1976)

562

Everyone is entitled to my opinion.

Madonna

563

CLASSIFIEDS
"Medium wanted for Halloween night seance with bowling after. Must be psychic and carry a 130 average."

"Exercise equipment for sale. Fat guy wants money for sofa."

from the Sonora Union-Democrat, *Oct. 29, 1990*

"Pretty redhead, 33, wants semi-traditional man. No nuevo-spiritualists, beach-walkers, minimum wagers, or first-date sexists. Prefer catcher's physique. 1B/3B/OF OK."   *from* L.A. Weekly, *Oct. 25, 1990*

564

It doesn't make any difference what temperature a room is, it's always room temperature.

Steven Wright

565

Things are always darkest just before they go pitch black.

from "I Spy"

566

It's time to open your parachute when cars look as big as ants. If ants look as big as cars, you've waited too long.

Ernst Luposchainsky III

567

An ounce of pretention is worth a pound of manure.

Steven E. Clark

568

Doing what you like is freedom; liking what you do is happiness.

Unknown

569

If you're lost in the woods, start playing solitaire with a pack of cards. Someone is sure to show up and tell you to put the red jack on the black queen.   *Unknown*

570

Inside every short person is a tall person doubled over in pain.   *Jeremy Kramer*

571

I would wish you the best of luck, but for all I know you're planning to kill me.   *Jackie Mason*

572

To lose a parent may be regarded as a misfortune; to lose both looks like carelessness.

Oscar Wilde (1856–1900)

Oscar Wilde was overdressed, pompous, snobbish, sentimental, and vain.   *Evelyn Waugh (1903–1966)*

573

Failing to prepare is preparing to fail.

John Wooden

574

I don't have false teeth. Do you think I'd buy teeth like these?
Carol Burnett

575

We owe something to extravagance, for thrift and adventure seldom go hand in hand.
Jennie Jerome Churchill (1854–1921)

576

To achieve the impossible dream, try going to sleep.
Joan Klempner

577

All marriages are mixed marriages.
Chantal Saperstein

578

What we need are new cliches.
Samuel Goldwyn (1882–1974)

579

When choosing a movie, the opinion of a dumb friend is better than the opinion of a smart critic.
George Leonard

580
Why don't they just get taller girls?
Fred Allen (1894–1956), at the ballet

581
Back in a minute . . .
—Godot

Graffito

582

For every action, there is an equal and opposite criticism.
Harrison's Postulate

583

Bad acting and dialogue make this a joy to watch.
Michael Weldon's review of the movie Jesse James Meets
Frankenstein's Daughter

584

Never spit in a man's face unless his moustache is on fire.
Henry Root

585

If you won't leave me alone, I'll find someone who will.
Unknown

586

Every day is a new beginning . . . and a chance to blow it.
Cathy Guisewite

587

Lead me not into temptation; I can find the way myself.
Rita Mae Brown

588

It's amazing that the amount of news that happens in the world every day always just exactly fits the newspaper.

Jerry Seinfeld

589

When I was thirty years old, my mother was still trying to have an abortion.

Jim Bailey as Phyllis Diller

590

We are all brothers beneath the belt.

Ralph Kramden (Jackie Gleason)

591

Friends are not necessarily the people you like best, they are merely the people who got there first.

Peter Ustinov

592

There's something about a closet that makes a skeleton restless.

Wilson Mizner (1876–1933)

593

Life is too short for traffic.

Dan Bellack

594

My mother-in-law had a pain below her left breast.
Turned out to be a trick knee.   *Phyllis Diller*

595

We must be the worst family in town. Maybe we should
move to a larger community.

Bart Simpson (Matt Groening)

596

Every California girl has lost at least one ovary,
And none of them has read *Madame Bovary*.

F. Scott Fitzgerald (1896–1940)

597

Societies that don't eat people are fascinated by those
that do.   *Ronald Wright*

598

What doesn't kill you makes you strong.
Friedrich Nietzsche (1844–1900)

Nietzsche was stupid and abnormal.
Leo Tolstoy (1828–1910)

599

In a hundred years? All new people.

Anne Lamott

600

Any act of charity shows a lack of judgment.

Martin Mull

601

Credo nonnullos hic mortuos esse.
   (I think several of the people here are dead.)
Sona is Latina loqueris.
   (Honk if you speak Latin.)
Mensa secunda mea flagrant!
   (My dessert is on fire!)
from Latin for All Occasions, *by Henry Beard*

602

Agoraphobia—Don't leave home without it.

Ben "Rivethead" Hamper

603

You don't realize what life is all about until you have found yourself lying on the edge of a great abcess.

Samuel Goldwyn (1882–1974)

604

Human beings are seventy percent water, and with some the rest is collagen.

Martin Mull

605

We would rather criticize ourselves than not talk about ourselves at all.

La Rochefoucauld (1613–1680)

606

My mind is important to me. It's where I spend most of my time.

Unknown

On leaving "The Tonight Show," I am reminded of the words of my mother when I left home as a young man: "How far do you think you'll get in that dress?"

Johnny Carson

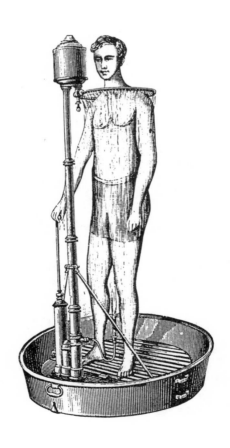

608

You know your party is out of control when people you don't even know ask you how the shower works.

Buddy Baron

609

In supermarkets, Soup For One is always eight aisles away from Party Mix.

Elayne Boosler

610

Where facts are few, experts are many.

Donald R. Gannon

611

A design is what the designer has when time and money run out.

James Poole

612

Everything is funny as long as it's happening to somebody else.

Will Rogers (1879–1935)

613

Tragedy is when I cut my finger. Comedy is when you fall in an open sewer and die.

Mel Brooks

614

Winter is reality, summer is illusion.

Toivo Pekkanen

615

You are not superior just because you see the world in an odious light.

Vicomte de Chateaubriand (1768–1848)

616

Keep your body warm and the rest of you will stay warm.

Scott Pugsley

617

TO HELL WITH YOU. OFFENSIVE LETTER FOLLOWS.

Telegram received by Sir Alec Douglas-Home

618

It's hard to feel morally superior to a person who gets up earlier than you do.

Mary Gordon

619

Better to be despised than forgotten.

from "St. Elsewhere"

620

My personal hobbies are reading, listening to music, and
silence.   *Dame Edith Sitwell (1887–1964)*

621

By the time I'd grown up, I naturally supposed that I'd be
grown up.   *Eve Babitz*

622

I'm so timid I was beaten up by Quakers.

Woody Allen

623

If three-fourths of the earth's surface is covered with
water, how come it's so hard to get to the beach?

Teressa Skelton

624

I have been selfish all my life, in practice, though not in
principle.   *Jane Austen (1775–1817)*

625

By whom?

Dorothy Parker (1893–1967) when told
she was outspoken

626

I know it's going to be a bad night when I see elderly women playing Frisbee with flattened road squirrels.

Johnny Carson

627

A person who trusts no one can't be trusted.

Jerome Blattner

628

When are you going to realize that if it doesn't apply to me it doesn't matter?

Candice Bergen as Murphy Brown

629

If you are afraid of being lonely, don't try to be right.

Jules Renard

6 3 0

Good girls go to heaven, and bad girls go everywhere.
Helen Gurley Brown

6 3 1

Nothing is ever accomplished by a reasonable man.
George Bernard Shaw (1856–1950)

6 3 2

Even the most useless person can serve as a bad example.
Unknown

6 3 3

Waste what you want not.

Russell Byrne

6 3 4

As long as there is algebra there will be prayer in school.
Larry Miller

6 3 5

The play had only one fault. It was kind of lousy.
James Thurber (1894–1961)

636

Misquotations are the only quotations that are never misquoted.   *Hesketh Pearson*

637

Bring down the curtain, the farce is over.
                    Last words of François Rabelais (1483–1553)

Part Four

Special Bonus Section

Compiler's note:

On what was without question the worst day of my life, I discovered that quote 270 in *The Other 637 Best Things Anybody Ever Said* (1984) was repeated as quote 285 in *The Third—And Possibly the Best—637 Best Things Anybody Ever Said* (1986). To make up for this error—which was the fault of the publishing industry, the Pope, your local cable operator, and the Pacific Gas & Electric Company—the following Bonus Quote is offered without additional charge.

BONUS QUOTE

Money is not the most important thing in the world. Love is. Fortunately, I love money.   *Jackie Mason*

Sources,
References,
and Notes

Readers who want 100,000 quotations at their finger-tips and who are interested in comparing wordings, ascriptions, translations, and sources should acquire for starters *A New Dictionary of Quotations on Historical Principles* (1952, 37,000 entries) by H. L. Mencken, *The Quotable Woman* (1978, 21,000 entries) by Elaine Partnow, and any of several editions of *Bartlett's Familiar Quotations* (16,000 entries). These and two dozen other secondary sources I sometimes consult are listed in *The 637 Best Things Anybody Ever Said* (1982) and *The Other 637 Best Things Anybody Ever Said* (1984). Two more recent tomes are the impressive *Macmillan Dictionary of Quotations* (1987, 20,000 entries), which was assembled by a team of five editors led by John Daintith, and the *Concise Columbia Dictionary of Quotations* (1990, 6,000 entries) by Robert Andrews.

While such heavyweight works simplify any compiler's

research, my principal sources remain my own reading, television watching, and eavesdropping, together with a network of friends and readers who let me know whenever they hear a good one. Bless them. May they regard the following citations ample reward.

The illustrations are selected from more than 25,000 in thirty collections of old linecuts, most of them published by Dover Publications. Leafing through them is like being happily lost in grandmother's attic.

Anyone devoted to one-liners owes a debt of gratitude to San Francisco's Herb Caen, who for an incredible fifty-two years has been writing a daily newspaper column that is as addictive as breakfast. He attracts smart remarks from wits and wags in a 400-mile radius and screens them with an unerring comic sense. Despite his half-century of service, Caen has stated that he will stay on the job until he collapses on his typewriter, his nose pressed against the "I" key.

The following notes on sources are sketchy and incomplete, in keeping with a book intended to be humorous rather than scholarly. If you can supply a missing ascription or source, if you know a zinger I missed, or if you want to take a stab at immortality by submitting one of your own lines, send me a note addressed as follows:

> Robert Byrne (Author)
> c/o Fawcett Books
> 201 E. 50th St.
> New York, NY 10022

1. EC in a letter to Byrne.
5. Thanks to Don Slattery.

8. JQ in *Gentlemen's Quarterly,* July 1990.
18. Thanks to Jonathan Benton.
21. Thanks to Gina Pierelli.
23. As quoted by Adair Lara in *The San Francisco Chronicle,* Jan. 4., 1991.
24. Thanks to Joan Kerr.
25. DW on the phone to Byrne.
26. From the play *Tru* by Jay Presson Allen.
27. JP to Byrne; JP is the daughter of Abigail Van Buren.
30. AEG in a letter to Byrne.
31. Thanks to Thomas D'Eletto.
32. LW is a standup comedian.
34–35. See 30.
36. KM is with The Kids in the Hall; as quoted in *Gentlemen's Quarterly,* July 1990.
38. Rita Rudner is a standup comedian.
41. DB on television series "Designing Women."
45. *Pickwick Papers,* chapter 23.
46. DP in *Dusk Before Fireworks.*
49. SS in his play *A Lie of the Mind.*
50. The strip appeared in February of 1991.
56. IM quoted in *The Observer,* Feb. 4, 1968.
64. Adapted from *The Best of Dear Abby,* 1981.
68. Thanks to Jonathan Benton.
69. TM is a British standup comedian.
72. HR in *The Rubaiyat of a Bachelor.*
73. SJL in *Unkempt Thoughts,* 1962; thanks to Lois Q. Novick.
75. CP is a college teacher in Philadelphia.
After 75. MI writing in *Mother Jones,* Sept. 1991.
79. CS is a standup comedian.
81. "The Tonight Show," Aug. 14, 1989.

83. JS as quoted by Herb Caen, *The San Francisco Chronicle,* Feb. 24, 1992.

88. Thanks to Don Slattery.

98. AH, thanks to Thomas D'Elletto.

108. LR is a standup comedian.

111. JK is a standup comedian.

115. CK as quoted in *Newsweek,* Oct. 28, 1991. CK is a psychiatrist who moonlights as a standup comedian.

116. LT as quoted in *The Quotable Woman,* 1978.

117. BR works at The Colorado Territorial Correctional Facility at Canyon City; thanks to Frank B. Miller.

118. JW in *The Secrets of Harry Bright.*

119. AB in his 1991 movie *Defending Your Life.*

120. V in *Thoughts of a Philosopher.*

122. MJH as quoted by Jon Carrol, *The San Francisco Chronicle,* Nov. 30, 1990.

124. LB is a mystery writer; thanks to Knox Burger.

130. EB is a standup comedian.

137. OL in the 1947 movie *Humoresque.*

138. AW in *The Vicious Circle.*

146. RL as quoted in *Gentlemen's Quarterly,* July 1990.

147. AM is a teenage standup comedian in Petaluma, Calif.

154. See 124.

159. Dame Edna is the stage persona of Australian comic Barry Humphries.

168. Blake Clark is a standup comedian.

169. ZS in a letter to Byrne.

170. Jeff Foxworthy, a standup comedian, in the trade paper *Just For Laughs,* April 1990.

171. MP was the wife of former Canadian Prime Minister Lester Pearson; thanks to Fritz T. Prugger.

176. See 115.

177. RGD is a bald British magistrate.

182. VW in *A Room of One's Own.*

185. RB is a fabulously wealthy stud.

191. JA in *Pride and Prejudice.*

193. AL in *The San Francisco Chronicle,* Dec. 19, 1990.

195. PS in *The San Francisco Chronicle,* Nov. 17, 1991.

197. CS on the television show "Evening at the Improv," Sept. 11, 1991.

201. EB in her syndicated column, Oct. 31, 1990.

202. Quoted by Mingo and Javna in their collection of quotes from television, *Primetime Proverbs,* 1989.

204. JS is a standup comedian.

206. JV in a letter to Byrne.

208. FL in *Metropolitan Life.*

210. M in *The San Francisco Chronicle,* Nov. 6, 1990.

212. IG quoted by Oriana Fallaci in *The New York Review of Books.*

213. KW is a British essayist.

217. B and R on *Classic Bob and Ray, 1946–1976,* cassette 2.

219. RR at The Third Annual Evening of Jewish Humor, San Francisco, May 20, 1990.

222. R as quoted in *Forbes,* Nov. 11, 1991.

223. JS as quoted by Herb Caen, *The San Francisco Chronicle,* Feb. 24, 1992.

226. BB as overheard by Byrne.

232. DB in *Dave Barry Turns 40,* 1990.

233. MK as quoted in *The Observer,* Aug. 20, 1978.

234. AJ in *The Diary of Alice James.*

237. RR as quoted in *Halliwell's Filmgoer's Companion,* 1988.

238. MM on "The Tonight Show," Sept. 13, 1990.

240. GD as quoted by Herb Caen, *The San Francisco Chronicle,* July 28, 1968.

242. JK to Mrs. Byrne (Cynthia Nelms).

256. IA in *Fantastic Voyage II: Destination Brain;* thanks to Andrew P. Campbell.

257. DB as quoted in *Newsweek,* Dec. 16, 1991.

258. BR as quoted in *The Macmillan Dictionary of Quotations,* 1989.

262. WA in his 1963 movie *What's Up Tiger Lily?*

264. EB in *The House in Paris.*

265. ND as quoted by Herb Caen, *The San Francisco Chronicle,* April 29, 1991.

266. P in *Apology;* thanks to Andrew P. Campbell.

268. RN accepting the presidential nomination, Aug. 8, 1963.

269. NC as quoted in *The Daily Telegraph,* July 17, 1973.

272. See 202.

276. JW as quoted by Herb Caen, *The San Francisco Chronicle,* Oct. 19, 1990.

280. Thanks to Jane Jordan.

283. RW in *The New Yorker,* Feb. 24, 1992.

286. CAU in a letter to Byrne.

287. MB in a letter to Byrne.

289. Screenplay by Ray Hyams.

293. AW, thanks to Adair Lara.

294. MS is a standup comedian.

295. AG to Mrs. Byrne.

296. SJ in *The Idler.*

After 296. OG as quoted by James Boswell in his biography of Samuel Johnson.

297. HC in *The San Francisco Chronicle,* Nov. 11, 1991.

298. Thanks to Craig Edgman.

299. GBS as quoted in *The Reader's Digest*, January 1992.
300. Thanks to Phillip Warren.
301. MM in *Gone With the Wind*.
307. Thanks to Jonathan Benton.
310. Thanks to William L. Hicks.
313. Thanks to Robert M. Guilbert, Sr.
316. BML as quoted in *Forbes*, Feb. 4, 1991.
317. Thanks to Denise Klahn.
318. ML as quoted by Tom Fitzgerald in *The San Francisco Chronicle*, April 16, 1991.
321. SR is a former pro football coach; thanks to Thomas J. Biemesderfer.
325. BH on "Bob Hope and Other Young Comedians," NBC, March 15, 1992.
326. JL on "The Tonight Show," June 19, 1990.
327. CJ, thanks to Craig Edgman.
328. MB, thanks to Kitty Sprague.
333. GB in *Wisdom of the 90's*, 1991.
334. SB in *Esquire*, June 1989.
337. FA as quoted in *Halliwell's Film Guide*, 1988.
339. DP-J in *Owls and Satyrs*.
344. ICD in a letter to *The San Francisco Chronicle*, January 1992.
348. IP in conversation with Mike Wallace.
349. HC in *The San Francisco Chronicle*, Dec. 18, 1990.
351. LL is a retired Chicago disk jockey; thanks to Gary Olsen.
352. GBS, thanks to Bill McCollough.
After 356. MI in *Mother Jones*, September 1991.
357. Thanks to Helen Giangregorio.
363. AH in *The Observer*, Aug. 17, 1969.

364. GG on the 75th anniversary of Edison's invention of the incandescent light in 1954.

367. TF is a professional basketball player.

368. GK on "The Prairie Home Companion," July 8, 1984.

369. PBS in *Peter Bell the Third*.

After 370. DHL in a letter to Aldous Huxley, Aug. 15, 1928.

371. TJ in a letter to John Page in 1786.

375. JG is a standup comedian.

376. JS in *Self* magazine, 1991.

378. DB as quoted in *Time,* July 3, 1989.

381. JQ, who says he tried standup comedy for one night, in *Gentlemen's Quarterly,* July 1990.

382. TC as quoted in the play *Tru* by Jay Presson Allen.

385. As quoted by Daniel J. Boorstin in *The Democratic Experience*.

386. As quoted by Thomas Swick in *The Fort Lauderdale Sun-Sentinel,* January 1990.

387. EB in *When You Look Like Your Passport Photo It's Time To Go Home,* 1991.

390. Thanks to Don Slattery.

392. FW is a standup comedian.

393. NR as quoted by Stephanie von Buchau in *The Pacific Sun,* June 1, 1990.

395. JT as quoted by Lowell Cohn, *The San Francisco Chronicle,* Jan. 21, 1992.

399. Thanks to R. T. Castleberry.

400. JM at the International Players Championship, March 17, 1992.

403. RC, thanks to Gordon Dewart.

406. TB is a standup comedian.

410. MK in *The Light Touch; How To Use Humor For Business Success,* 1991.

414. Thanks to Jonathan Benton.

418. SS in *The Marin Independent Journal,* Feb. 16, 1992.

419. KW in *How To Survive Children.*

425. SDO addressing the American Bar Association convention, August 1991.

428. HC in *The San Francisco Chronicle,* Jan. 17, 1992.

436. The C and H comic strip ran on Nov. 8, 1989; thanks to Chris Querry and Len Neff.

439. KM as quoted by George Seldes in *The Great Quotations,* 1960.

440. L as quoted by George Seldes in *The Great Quotations,* 1960.

441. L in *The State and Revolution.*

443. FZ in *The Real Frank Zappa Book,* 1989.

444. MR as quoted in *Newsweek,* Feb. 6, 1990.

445. MT in *M,* January 1992.

446. NB as quoted in *Never Trust a Calm Dog* by Tom Parker, 1990.

448. AS as quoted in *Forbes,* Dec. 9, 1991.

450. V in *Notebooks.*

452. JC on "The Tonight Show," Sept. 11, 1991.

453. V in a letter to Damilaville, April 1, 1766.

454. HB in *The Entertainer,* an English language newspaper in Spain, Feb. 16, 1990.

457. Thanks to Jonathan Benton.

458. TL on a television commercial, Jan. 28, 1992.

461. EO as quoted by Erica Jong in *Fear of Flying.*

464. JG as quoted by Herb Caen in *The San Francisco Chronicle,* April 19, 1990.

466. AS in *The San Francisco Examiner,* Nov. 4, 1990.

467. JC on "The Tonight Show," Aug. 17, 1990.

470. HLM as quoted in *The New Yorker,* Feb. 24, 1992.

471. JR in *Deadline,* 1991.

476. Also said about Herbert Hoover, according to Herb Caen.

479. PAL as quoted by Herb Caen, *The San Francisco Chronicle,* Feb. 3, 1992.

480. JC on "The Tonight Show," Sept. 11, 1991.

481. DQ speaking in Fresno, Calif., January 1992.

486. MF as recalled by the present Governor of Texas, Ann Richards.

489. FW on "Fernwood 2-Night."

493. GW is a standup comedian.

494. V was referring to British Admiral Byng, who was executed for failing to defeat the French at Minorca in 1757.

495. IG at a press conference on Oct. 19, 1971.

499. CL as quoted in the comedian's trade paper *Just For Laughs,* December 1990.

502. Quoted by Herb Caen, *The San Francisco Chronicle,* March 16, 1992.

505. DS at The Third Annual Evening of Jewish Humor, San Francisco, May 20, 1990.

507. CM as quoted in *Forbes,* Feb. 3, 1992.

508. HB in an 1835 letter; thanks to Frederick Gabrielsen.

509. KK as quoted by Ethan Canin in a talk at the Marin County Day School in California, Oct. 23, 1991.

510. See 509.

511. C in *The Blue Lantern,* 1949.

512. EH as quoted by Malvin Wold in *The Journal of the*

Writers Guild of America West, May 1991; thanks to Joe Gores.

513. JJ in *Lesbian Nation; The Feminist Solution,* 1973.

514. Thanks to Don Slattery.

516. JB on the San Francisco radio station KNBR, Nov. 13, 1990.

517. CD in his *Autobiography.*

518. PB is a British theater director.

520. GBS in *Dramatic Opinions and Essays.*

525. LG in a letter to Byrne.

526. SB, thanks to Mel Helms.

527. JBB in his syndicated column, June 9, 1991.

528. Thanks to Leah Garchik.

529. RW in *The Strange Necessity.*

532. PL, a British poet, in *A Study of Reading Habits.*

537. Adapted from DC's cartoon strip *Winthrop,* Jan. 20, 1992.

538. DW as quoted by Herb Caen, *The San Francisco Chronicle,* Dec. 13, 1991.

539. As quoted by Tom Fitzgerald in *The San Francisco Chronicle,* Jan. 24, 1992.

543. Adapted from a *Peanuts* cartoon strip, June 19, 1991.

545. As quoted by Adair Lara, *The San Francisco Chronicle,* Feb. 6, 1992.

547. BS in a letter to Byrne.

554. SM in *Of Human Bondage.*

557. See 159.

565. See 202.

566. EL in *Never Trust a Calm Dog* by Tom Parker, 1990.

568. Thanks to Don Slattery.

572. OW in *The Importance of Being Earnest.*

After 572. EW in *Harper's Bazaar,* Nov. 1930.

577. CS, thanks to Linda Strauss.

578. SG as quoted in *Goldwyn: A Biography* by A. Scott Berg.

579. GL in conversation with Byrne.

580. Thanks to Kathy Showen.

583. MW in *The Psychotronic Encyclopedia of Film,* 1989.

584. HR in *The Letters of Henry Root,* 1978.

587. RMB, thanks to Thomas D'Eletto.

596. FSF in *The Crack-Up.*

597. RW, thanks to Thomas D'Eletto.

599. AL in her novel *All New People.*

603. SG as quoted in *The Moguls* by Norman Zierold, 1969.

605. LR in *Maxims,* 1665.

607. AR, thanks to Andrew P. Campbell.

608. BB as quoted by Herb Caen, *The San Francisco Chronicle,* March 18, 1992.

610. DRG in a letter to Byrne.

611. JP, Chief Architect for Disneyland, in a letter to Byrne.

613. MB, thanks to Chris Querry.

618. MG in *Final Payments.*

619. Thanks to Katherine Simonetti.

622. WA in his 1973 movie *Sleeper.*

623. TS to Byrne.

627. JB in a letter to Byrne.

629. JR, thanks to Tim Newlin.

631. GBS, thanks to Vikki L. Chesin.

632. Thanks to William L. Hicks.

635. JT as quoted in *The Macmillan Dictionary of Quotations,* 1989.

Index of Authors

Index of Authors

Index of Subjects and Key Words

About the Author

ROBERT BYRNE radiates a quiet strength and trustworthiness that have endeared him to a generation of discriminating readers. Before turning to writing, he was a full-time lover of country, family, and pets as well as a successful salesman of home barber kits. A tall, rangy man with quick hands and feet, he plans to spend the coming season in Spain playing professional basketball, having rejected the latest offer from the Petaluma Poltroons.